W9-BMQ-958

CORAL REEFS

Written by **Jenny Wood**

Consultant Roger Hammond
Director of Living Earth

Scholastic, Inc.
New York Toronto London Auckland Sydney

Copyright © Two-Can Publishing Ltd, 1991

Printed and bound in Hong Kong

All rights reserved. No part of this publication may be reproduced, or
stored in a retrieval system or transmitted in any form or by any means
electronic, mechanical, photocopying, recording or otherwise, without
written permission of the copyright holder, Scholastic Inc, 730 Broadway,
New York, NY 10003, USA

First published in Great Britain by Two-Can Publishing Ltd
346 Old Street London EC1V 9NQ

This edition published by Scholastic Inc,
730 Broadway, New York, NY 10003, USA

ISBN 0-590-74256-6

Photographic credits:
Cover (front) Planet Earth Pictures (back) Bruce Coleman; p.5 Ardea; p.6 (top) Ardea (bottom left) Ardea; 6/7 Bruce Coleman; p.7 Ardea; p.9
Planet Earth Pictures; p.10 Zefa; p.11 Ardea; p.12/13\Bruce Coleman; p.14 (top) Ardea (bottom) Bruce Coleman; p.15 Robert Harding; p.16 (top)
Planet Earth Pictures (bottom) Zefa; p.17 (top) Oxford Scientific Films (bottom) Zefa; p.18 Bruce Coleman; p.20 Robert Harding; p.21 Bruce
Coleman; p.22 Oxford Scientific Films; p.23 Oxford Scientific Films.

Illustration Credits:
All illustrations by Francis Mosley except p.24-28 Martin Sailsbury/Linda Rogers Associates.

CONTENTS

All words marked in **bold** can be found in the glossary

WHAT IS A CORAL REEF?

In the clear, shallow waters of the world's warm seas, huge reefs of orange, yellow and purple coral can be found. The corals come in all forms, shaped like branching trees, tiny pipes or saucers. They are ridges of limestone, formed by millions of tiny animals called coral polyps.

The polyps that build the reefs are known as stony corals. They live together in colonies. **Cells** on the outside of the polyps' bodies collect a chemical called calcium carbonate from the sea water. Calcium carbonate hardens to form limestone, and this grows into a protective shell around each polyp. When the polyps die, their shells remain. As new polyps grow on the old limestone shells, the reef becomes larger.

▶ Coral reefs are often described as underwater gardens. They are colorful, fascinating places, and provide a home for many sea creatures.

A new coral reef begins with a single, tiny polyp called a **planula**. Planulae are produced from the eggs of some types of female stony coral polyps which have been fertilized by **sperm** from a male polyp. They swim through the water until they find a hard surface on which to rest. As soon as a planula is settled, it begins producing limestone.

Once the building of
a new reef has been
started, the polyps begin
to bud. Small, knob-like
growths appear on the
body of each adult
polyp. These gradually
develop into
independent polyps,
and so the reef begins
to increase in size.

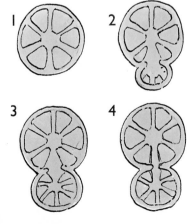

A CLOSER LOOK AT CORAL

There are more than 2,500 **species** of coral. About 650 of these are the reef-building stony corals whose limestone shells and skeletons form the basic structure of a coral reef. But other types of coral grow on or near a reef, too, though their colonies are smaller in size. These are the colorful soft corals.

Soft corals do not produce limestone shells to protect their bodies. Instead, they have horn-like skeletons, which are strengthened by tiny needles of limestone called **spicules.** Soft corals can bend and sway in the water.

▼ Corals come in a huge variety of colors. Some are very bright, like this Cave Coral, and some are even fluorescent.

6

▶ Gorgonian corals develop colonies made up of long, thin branches which sway in the ocean **currents**. These corals have an internal skeleton made out of a material called gorgonin.

◀ Can you see the mouths of those hard coral polyps?

▼ Coral polyps eat tiny sea creatures known as **zooplankton**. They capture their food using stinging cells on their tentacles. When zooplankton brush past a polyp's tentacles, the threads shoot out and stun the tiny animals. The tentacles then carry the zooplankton into the polyp's mouth.

WHERE CORAL REEFS ARE FOUND

Reef-building stony corals cannot live in water that is colder than 18°C, so the world's coral reefs are found in the warm seas that lie on either side of the Equator. Corals always develop in clear, shallow water which is no more than 45 m deep, so many coral reefs are situated near land.

Scientists believe that the stony corals choose clear, shallow water in which to develop because of their special relationship with a tiny form of **algae** known as

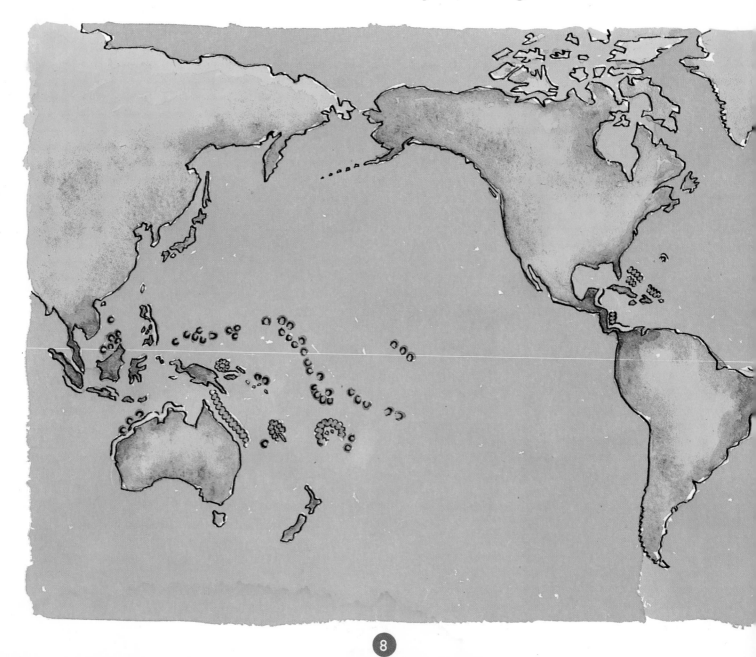

zooxanthellae. Zooxanthellae live inside the cells of the coral polyps' bodies. They use energy from sunlight to make food and, as they do this, they provide the polyps with nourishment. Sunlight does not reach into deep ocean water, so the zooxanthellae need to remain close to the surface. The polyps, in turn, need the food provided by the zooxanthellae, so they too must stay in shallow water.

▲ Many different types of coral live clustered together. These corals are in the Red Sea.

◀ The world's coral reefs.

Key to map

～～～	**Fringe reef**
～～～	**Barrier reef**
⟩ⵔⵔⵔⵔ	**Coral atoll**

FRINGE REEFS AND BARRIER REEFS

Fringe reefs form a border or fringe of coral along a shoreline. They grow on the shelves of rock that extend from the shores of islands or continents into the sea. A fringe reef is separated from the land by a narrow stretch of water which is shallow enough to wade across when the tide is out.

Barrier reefs also grow parallel to the land, but are separated from

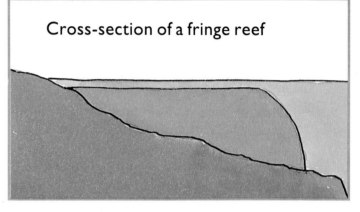

Cross-section of a fringe reef

▼ It is easy to see the coral under the clear water from the air.

the shoreline by a larger area of calm water called a lagoon. They act as a barrier between the lagoon and the waters of the open sea.

The world's largest and best-known barrier reef is the Great Barrier Reef, off the northeastern coast of Australia. It stretches for 2,027 km, and parts of it lie over 160 km from the coast. Like most barrier reefs, the Great Barrier Reef is made up of smaller reefs separated by channels of water.

▶ Heron Island is one of the thousands of islands with fringe reefs which form part of Australia's Great Barrier Reef.

DID YOU KNOW?

● The Great Barrier Reef is the largest single structure ever built by living creatures.

● About 400 different species of coral grow on the Great Barrier Reef.

● Scientists believe that the Great Barrier Reef began forming 30 million years ago.

● The foundations of the Great Barrier Reef lie over 150m below the surface of the water, over three times the maximum depth at which reef-building corals grow. Scientists believe that the reef was originally a fringe reef, which sank as movements of the earth's **crust** lowered the level of the sea bed.

CORAL ATOLLS

Coral atolls are the most unusual type of reef. An atoll is a ring of coral which surrounds nothing but water.

The 19th century scientist, Charles Darwin, was the first person to explain how atolls developed. He believed that an atoll started life as a fringe reef surrounding a **volcanic island**. Over thousands of years, movements in the earth's crust caused changes in the level of the ocean floor, and the island, including its surrounding reef, began to sink. New coral continued to form on the top of the reef, so once the island was covered by the sea, only the reef remained.

Sometimes coral atolls develop into coral islands. A thin layer of sand covers the reef, and trees and plants grow from seeds carried by birds or the wind.

▼The Maldive Islands in the Indian Ocean are coral atolls. Most coral islands are no more than six meters high, and some are less than one meter above the water. They are in constant danger of being flooded by heavy seas caused by tropical storms.

How a coral atoll is formed.

1 A fringe reef grows around a volcanic island.

2 As the island begins to sink, the stretch of water between it and the coral reef widens. The reef is now a barrier reef.

3 The island disappears completely beneath the surface, and a coral atoll now surrounds a shallow lagoon. Channels between the stretches of coral connect the lagoon with the open sea.

CORAL REEF CREATURES

Coral reefs are full of creatures. No other underwater **habitat** is home to fish of so many different species. In one area of the Great Barrier Reef, about 2,000 different species have been recorded.

Most coral reef fish are brilliantly colored. Their bodies often have unusual shapes and are decorated with stripes, spots and other markings. These allow them to blend in with their surroundings and hide easily from their enemies.

Many of the creatures and plants which live in and around the coral reef are dependent on each other for food and shelter. One of the most

▲ The Harlequin tusk fish has teeth outside its mouth like tusks.

▶ This anemone is surrounded by clown fish and Damsel fish.

unusual relationships is that between the clown fish and the sea anemone. The tentacles of the sea anemone release poison at the slightest touch. But the clown fish are not affected by the poison. They lay their eggs near the anemone's base and rear their young among the swaying tentacles. They leave this shelter only to find food.

The anemone benefits from the partnership by eating the left-overs of the clown fish's meals. The clown fish may also attract other fish to the anemone, which the anemone then gobbles up.

▲ Angelfish are among the most colorful reef-dwelling fish. They have narrow, streamlined bodies, and dart with ease through the coral.

SPONGES AND STARFISH

Many creatures other than fish make their home on a coral reef. Prickly starfish and sea urchins move slowly across the reef, using the suckers on the undersides of their bodies to grip the surface. Fierce marine snails hide their soft bodies within beautifully patterned shells. Clams and oysters lie buried in the sand or attached to the reef limestone, opening their shells from time to time to take in food. Colorful crabs hide in the nooks and crannies of the reef, and tiny shrimps swim through the shallow water. Sponges of all shapes, colors and sizes live among the coral.

▲ The blue starfish grows up to 40cm from the tip of one arm to the tip of another.

◀ Under each arm, a starfish has a row of suction disks which it uses to move along the coral. At the tip of each arm is an eyespot which is sensitive to light, although the starfish moves more by feel than sight.

Some of the reef creatures grow to an enormous size. Giant clams, for example, can weigh more than 230 kg and measure over one meter in length. They feed on tiny plants and animals which they filter from the sea water.

▲Seahorses belong to a group of fish known as 'tube-mouths'. They hold themselves steady in the water by hooking their tails round the coral.

▶There are more than 5,000 different species of sponge of all shapes and sizes. Sponges are animals, although for many years they were classed as plants. Sponges attach themselves to the hard surface of the reef. They feed by drawing water into their bodies, then sieving out the tiny plants and animals that they eat.

DID YOU KNOW?

● A starfish's favorite meal is a shellfish such as a clam, oyster, scallop or mussel. The starfish wraps itself around the shellfish, places its mouth over the seam between the two shells and pulls hard. As the shells begin to come apart, the starfish turns its stomach inside out through its mouth and pushes it through the opening. The starfish's stomach surrounds the shellfish's soft body and gobbles it up!

● If a starfish loses part of its body during a fight with another underwater creature, the lost body part will grow again. The blue starfish can grow a whole new body from just a single arm and part of the central disk.

CORAL IN DANGER

A giant starfish, known as the crown-of-thorns, has caused terrible destruction to many of the world's coral reefs. The crown-of-thorns eats coral polyps, but instead of nibbling small areas and leaving enough living coral for new polyps to grow, the crown-of-thorns strips the coral bare until only a white skeleton of dead coral remains.

About 30 years ago, scientists began noticing that the world population of these starfish was increasing. Large groups of them began feeding on reefs in the Pacific Ocean, and on the Great Barrier Reef.

Some scientists believe that human beings may have caused the problem. One of the few animals which eats the crown-of-thorns is the triton, a large marine snail with a beautiful shell. Shell collectors have reduced the number of tritons in the sea, and may have allowed the crown-of-thorns to increase in number. Other scientists think that population explosions occur from time to time, as part of a natural cycle, and are best left alone.

◀ A crown-of-thorns feeding on the polyps of a stony coral. The crown-of-thorns has 16 arms, each covered with prickly spines.

Each crown-of-thorns can devour about two square meters of coral a week. In the space of two and a half years, thousands of them destroyed almost all the living coral along a 38 km stretch of reef surrounding the Pacific island of Guam. Areas of Australia's Great Barrier Reef are now in danger.

MAKE A CORAL REEF

Make you own minature coral reef and watch the fish swim back and forth, then disappear.

You will need:
- 3 pieces of cardboard
- felt pens or paint
- scissors
- glue

1 Color one piece of cardboard blue for the sea, and draw some fish swimming in it.

2 On the edge of the second piece of cardboard, draw a coral reef. Cut out the center.

3 On the third piece of cardboard draw a fish.

4 Cut out the fish shape and glue it onto a strip of cardboard you have colored blue.

5 Glue the cut-out piece of cardboard to the blue background. Glue along the top and bottom edges only.

6 Push the strip of cardboard with the fish between the two pieces of cardboard. Pull it back and forth and watch the fish move, then disappear behind the coral.

DANGER FROM PEOPLE

Many of the world's coral reefs are popular tourist attractions. Tourist boats **pollute** the water with gasoline and oil. Those who dive down to the reef may damage the coral by stepping on it or scraping it with their diving tanks. Others may break off pieces of coral to take home, although in most places it is now illegal to collect coral.

Over-fishing is another problem. If too many fish are taken from one reef or one part of a reef, the whole balance of life on the reef can change. In some parts of the Caribbean so many algae eating fish were harvested from the sea that the algae could not be kept under control. The algae swamped the coral and the reef died.

Sewage from towns and cities and poisonous waste materials from

▼ Many corals, such as this huge brain coral, have been vandalized by tourists.

▲ Painted coral gathered from the Great Barrier Reef is sold to tourists.

factories may end up in the water surrounding a coral reef. The dirtier and more polluted the water becomes, the more difficult it is for coral polyps to survive.

Sometimes people clear areas of land near a coastline to make way for crops or houses. The soil is washed into the sea and covers the coral in a layer of mud, which blocks out the sunlight. The zooxanthellae, which provide the coral polyps with nourishment, die out, so the polyps die. The reef is then deserted by all the other living creatures who depend on it for food and shelter.

DID YOU KNOW?

● Every weekday, an average of 3000 people visit the coral reefs in Pennekamp Coral Reef State Park, Florida, USA. On warm summer weekends, that number may rise to 6000 per day! Between 1984 and 1989, as tourists swarmed to Pennekamp, the amount of damage to the coral increased by 300%! It is now likely that some of the reefs will have to be closed to visitors to allow the coral time to recover.

SCIENCE AT WORK

Marine biologists who study the plants and animals that live in the sea have learned many things about human life from them. Studies of sea urchins, for example, have provided information about the way in which a human baby grows and develops inside its mother's womb. Experiments on squids may help us understand how messages are sent from the human brain to various parts of the body.

Many sea creatures produce substances which are helpful to human beings.

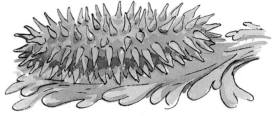

Coral, sponges, sea cucumbers and seaweed all contain materials which can be used to treat illnesses, including cancer.

Some sponges produce substances that can be used to treat skin infections, food and blood poisoning, and pneumonia.

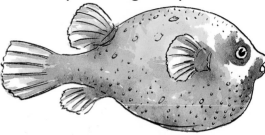

The poisons produced from certain kinds of shellfish and puffer fish are powerful **anesthetics,** far more powerful than the drugs doctors use at the moment.

Marine biologists believe that many of these materials will eventually be used in the preparation of medicine.

▲This platform has been set up as a base for marine biologists studying the reef.

▶ Divers divide off an area of reef for close study of the plant and animal life.

SHIPWRECK

The storm had been raging for three days. At first we were allowed to help the adults on deck, but since the Seaspray's mast had broken yesterday, we had been told to stay in the cabin. My sister Carrie would not stop sniffling and, to tell the truth, I was cold, wet and miserable enough to want to do the same. However, Mom had told me to look after the kids while the adults battled the elements up top, so I gave it my best.

Suddenly the cabin door flung open and Mom came in. She banged the door closed behind her, shutting out the darkness and

howling wind, and stood there, a mass of dripping yellow rainsuits.

"Now listen carefully," she began, "Dad thinks we're about to hit a reef, so we'll have to be ready to abandon ship."

She turned to me. "Sue, you're in charge. Get together some food and the first aid kit. As soon as I call, everyone up on deck. And hang on to one another!"

With another flurry of rainsuits and water, she left the cabin.

Just when I finished sorting out a bag of essentials, and helped Carrie and Luke into their life-jackets, I heard a booming noise and then felt a grinding thud. Mom's shout sounded very faint, but I hustled the kids up on deck. The wind and rain whipped around us, but the boat lay still, stuck firmly on the coral.

Dad had left the raft down on the sheltered side of the Seaspray and Luke's mother was already in it, ready to help us down. Quickly, we all got in and Dad pushed off from the yacht and zipped the raft's cover over us.

For a while the raft tossed and turned, like the weirdest roller-coaster ride I have ever been on. Then, all of a sudden, it stilled.

"We must have reached the lagoon," said Dad.

He unzipped the cover of the raft, and, in the moonlight, we could see a white beach before us. The wind and rain were unrelenting, but the water, sheltered from the ocean current by the reef, was quite calm. Dad unclipped the oars and Mom and he began to row towards the moonlit shore.

The next morning, I awoke to find myself on a beach straight out of a travel brochure. The dazzling white sand was lined with palm trees and the sun shone on the clear blue waves.

Dad was already awake.

"Come on!" he called to me. "Let's see what it's like."

We walked inland, where the ground rose steadily into a high hill. From the top, we could see the whole island, surrounded by the peaceful lagoon and then the ridge of coral. Beyond that lay the Pacific Ocean, tossing up white waves against the coral. I could hardly believe that this peaceful expanse of water was the same that had ripped our yacht to pieces only yesterday.

"Wow!" I said. "We're real, live castaways!"

"Not for long, I hope," said Dad. "I managed to send out a distress call before we abandoned ship. But, in the meantime, let's enjoy this adventure."

"Hey, Carrie, Luke," I yelled, as I ran back down to the beach. "Let's go and look for buried treasure!"

TRUE OR FALSE?

Which of these facts are true and which ones are false?
If you have read this book carefully, you will know the answers.

1 There are four different types of coral reef.

2 Most fish that live in and around a coral reef have brightly colored bodies.

3 Scientists who study life in the sea are called marine biologists.

4 The polyps which build coral reefs are known as soft corals.

5 Most coral reefs are found in cold seas.

6 A barrier reef is separated from the shore by an area of calm water called a lagoon.

7 Sponges are a type of underwater plant.

8 The effects of tourism are destroying many of the world's coral reefs.

9 Coral polyps capture food by using the stinging cells on their tentacles.

10 An atoll is a type of fish.

11 The crown-of-thorns is a type of coral polyp which eats starfish.

12 Many of the creatures and plants which live in and around a coral reef depend on each other for food and shelter.

Answers: 1 False; 2 True; 3 True; 4 False; 5 False; 6 True; 7 False; 8 True; 9 True; 10 False; 11 False; 12 True

GLOSSARY

Algae are a group of tiny plants which provide food for many sea creatures. There are about 25,000 different types of algae.

Anesthetics are drugs used in medicine to prevent a person feeling pain. Anesthetics work by causing loss of feeling in an area of the body or in the whole body. The effects of an anesthetic last for only a short time.

Barrier reef is a type of coral reef separated from a shoreline by an area of calm water called a lagoon.

Reef

Lagoon

Cells are sometimes called 'units of life'. All living things are made up of cells. Some animals and plants have only one cell; others are made up of many cells. In many-celled creatures, each cell has a particular job to do.

Coral atoll is a ring-shaped coral reef which often surrounds nothing but water. Coral atolls may develop into coral islands as trees and plants begin to grow from seeds carried by the wind, by birds, or on the ocean currents.

Crust is the name given to earth's thin surface layer. It is made up of huge, thick slabs of rock called plates which float on the hot, liquid rock of the mantle, the next layer.

Currents are movements of water, each travelling in a particular direction. There are many currents in the world's oceans.

Fringe reef is a type of coral reef which forms a border or fringe of coral along a shoreline. A fringe reef is separated from the land by a narrow stretch of water.

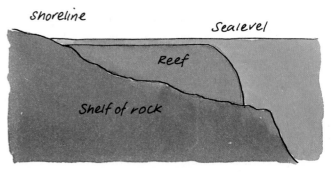

shoreline

Sealevel

Reef

Shelf of rock

Habitat is the word used to describe the natural home of a plant, animal, insect or person.

Mucus is a clear, thick, slimy fluid produced in various parts of a creature's body.

Planula is a single, young coral polyp. The plural of the word is planulae.

Pollute means to make something dirty. Earth's water is being polluted by all the human and industrial waste which is dumped into rivers, lakes and seas.

Species is the word used to describe a group of animals or plants which are alike in certain ways.

Sewage is water which contains waste materials produced by humans. Most sewage eventually flows into rivers, lakes or seas. In many countries, sewage is treated beforehand, to remove harmful chemicals and bacteria. But in some countries, sewage is not treated, and so the rivers, lakes and seas are polluted, causing harm to the creatures which live there as well as to humans.

Sperm are male sex cells which, when joined with female sex cells, are capable of producing a baby or young creature.

Spicules are tiny needles of limestone which strengthen the bodies of soft corals.

Tentacles are the flexible, tube-like parts of a coral polyp's body which surround its mouth and are used to collect food. Other sea creatures, such as sea anemones, also have tentacles.

Volcanic island is an island formed by an underwater volcano. Each time the volcano erupts, it grows in size until its tip lies above sea level. The tip of the volcano is the volcanic island.

Zooplankton are tiny creatures which float through the water and are eaten by coral polyps.

Zooxanthellae are a type of algae which live inside the bodies of coral polyps and provide them with nourishment. Zooxanthellae use energy from sunlight to make food, and so they must live in clear, shallow water where the sunlight can reach them.

INDEX